**Managing Editor**
Ina Massler Levin, M.A.

**Editor-in-Chief**
Sharon Coan, M.S. Ed.

**Illustrator**
Howard Chaney

**Cover Artist**
Barb Lorseyedi

**Art Director**
CJae Froshay

**Art Coordinator**
Kevin Barnes

**Product Manager**
Phil Garcia

**Imaging**
Temo Parra

**Publisher**
Mary D. Smith, M.S. Ed.

# Reading Comprehension

### Practice Makes Perfect

### GRADE 5

**Author**

*Teacher Created Resources Staff*

*Teacher Created Resources, Inc.*
6421 Industry Way
Westminster, CA 92683
www.teachercreated.com

**ISBN: 978-0-7439-3366-7**

*©2002 Teacher Created Resources, Inc.*
Reprinted, 2011
Made in U.S.A.

# Table of Contents

# Introduction

The old adage "practice makes perfect" can really hold true for your child and his or her education. The more practice and exposure your child has with concepts being taught in school, the more success he or she is likely to find. For many parents, knowing how to help their children may be frustrating because the resources may not be readily available.

As a parent it is also difficult to know where to focus your efforts so that the extra practice your child receives at home supports what he or she is learning in school.

This book has been written to help parents and teachers reinforce basic skills with children. *Practice Makes Perfect: Reading Comprehension* gives practice with reading and answering questions to help fully comprehend what is read. The exercises in this book can be done sequentially or can be taken out of order, as needed.

After reading the story the questions can be answered either by circling the answers or by reproducing and using the fill-in answer sheets found on pages 46 and 47. The practice tests, one for each of the areas of reading, can be bubbled in on the answer pages that are provided for each test.

The standards or objectives that follow will be met or reinforced by completing the practice pages included in this book. These standards and objectives are similar to the ones required by your state and school district. These standards and objectives are appropriate for the fifth grade.

- The student will demonstrate competence in making simple predictions about what is being read.
- The student will demonstrate competence in using various reading strategies to read the stories and answer the questions.
- The student will demonstrate competence in finding the main idea in a story, making inferences and predictions.
- The student will be familiar with different types of reading (fiction, nonfiction, informational).
- The student will be able to use context clues and other aides to determine the meaning of a word.

## How to Make the Most of This Book

Here are some useful ideas for making the most of this book:

- Set aside a specific place in your home to work on this book. Keep it neat and tidy with necessary materials readily available.
- Set up a certain time of day to work on these practice pages to establish consistency, or look for times in you and your child's day or week that are less hectic and conducive to practicing skills.
- Keep all practice sessions with your child positive and constructive. If the mood becomes frustrated or tense, set the book aside and look for another time to practice with your child. Forcing your child to perform will not help. Do not use this book as a punishment.
- Help beginning readers with instructions.
- Review the work your child has done.
- Pay attention to the areas in which your child has the most difficulty. Provide extra guidance and exercises in those areas.
- Read aloud with your child and ask reading comprehension questions.

# Branding Day

Ivan followed his dad out to the pasture. He knew what time of year it was. It was not an easy task, but every May, Ivan would help his dad round up the cattle and herd them into the yards. Dad would already have the brand in the fire, so it would be hot. Once the cows were lined up, Ivan would push the first reluctant cow into the squeeze gate, close the fence behind the cow, and motion to his dad. Dad would hurry over, with the hot brand in his gloved hands, and shove it at the cow's hindquarters.

Ivan was never entirely comfortable with branding time. He helped his dad every year, however, because he wanted to learn as much about ranching as he could. He liked working outside with the cows, but the heat branding always bothered him. The brand was red hot when Dad touched it to the cow's hide, and Ivan always thought it looked very painful. Sometimes the brand would get infected, and Dad would have to go out to the field, find the cow, and clean the wound with alcohol every day.

"Ready to brand the cows, Ivan?" his dad asked. "We're going to try something different this year. I looked into freeze branding over the winter. It's safer and easier than heat branding. They tell me the cows won't be as bothered by it either."

Ivan looked at his dad and smiled. He was always glad when they understood each other.

After they had herded all the cattle into the yard, Ivan led the first one to the squeeze gate. Dad set a foam cooler on the ground. When he lifted the lid off, white vapor, like fog, rose out of the cooler. Dad explained that the liquid nitrogen was about 320 degrees below zero. The vapor was nitrogen gas that had been warmed by the outside air. He put the brand into the liquid nitrogen to freeze it. Then he took some battery-operated clippers out of a pocket and sheared a section of hair off the back of the cow. The cow grunted nervously. Then, Dad pulled a bottle of alcohol out of his other pocket and poured some onto the side of the cow's hindquarter.

"That's to help the cold transfer to the skin of the cow," he explained. "It also cleans the area, so there's little chance of infection. Now, watch," he told Ivan, who had been holding the rope.

Dad lifted the brand out of the nitrogen cooler. The four-inch J.R. symbol of the brand was frosted over, as moisture froze to the cold iron. Ivan knew the letters were the two initials of his parents, Janeane and Robert. No one else used exactly the same brand, so the different ranchers could tell their herds apart.

Dad pushed the brand against the cow's flank. Ivan was prepared for a hissing sound, but there was almost no sound at all. The cow leaned a little away from the brand, but it was nothing like how they reacted when they were heat branded.

"That's all there is to it," he said. "Now, let this cow out to the yard, and bring me another."

# Branding Day *(Cont.)*

**After reading the story, answer the questions.  Circle the correct answer.**

1. How did Ivan learn about branding cattle?
    a. His best friend owned a cattle ranch.
    b. He read about it in a book.
    c. He did the branding with his uncle every year.
    d. He helped his father with the branding.

2. Why was Ivan uncomfortable with branding time?
    a. He thought the branding was painful for the cattle.
    b. It was usually very cold outside when it was branding time.
    c. He was not very interested in learning about ranching.
    d. He thought the cows might hurt him.

3. Why did Ivan smile when his father explained about freeze branding?
    a. Ivan was eager to learn about this new technique in branding.
    b. Ivan would get his first chance to do the branding himself.
    c. Ivan would prove to his father that he would be a good rancher someday.
    d. Ivan knew his father understood how he felt about the heat branding.

4. The reader can tell that Ivan's father was
    a. always in a hurry.
    b. unhappy with Ivan.
    c. a traditional rancher.
    d. caring and thoughtful.

5. You can tell from this story that
    a. Ivan would never help his father with branding time again.
    b. Ivan was happier about branding time than he had been before.
    c. Ivan could do the branding by himself.
    d. Ivan's father did not like the new method of branding.

6. Which sentence could best be added to the end of the first paragraph?
    a. Ivan would refuse to bring the next cow into the pen.
    b. Ivan would encourage the cow to run out of the gate before it could get branded.
    c. Ivan would take the branding iron and brand the cow himself.
    d. Ivan would squeeze his eyes closed for a few seconds each time.

# Dad's Haircut

Tony's father was a busy man. Every day he woke up at 4 a.m., fed the sheep in the barn, and opened the gate to the pasture. Then he drove to his job in the city. When he came home at night, he would make sure the sheep were safe in the barn. He was known as a "weekend farmer" because he had both a small farm and a regular job in the city. But Tony knew his father really had two full-time jobs. This meant Tony's father was always so busy that he rarely got a haircut. His hair was so big and curly that Tony's mother often joked, "Don't get too close to the sheep, or they might think you have a stack of hay on your head and take a nibble!"

Today, Tony's job was to get the sheep ready for shearing before his father got home. They were going to shear every sheep on the farm, even if it took all night. He was oiling the electric shears when his father's car pulled into the driveway. He saw his father looking uncertainly at his bushy hair in the car mirror.

"What's wrong, Dad?" asked Tony.

"Oh, nothing, son," replied his father, pulling his briefcase out of the car. "Just my city job, that's all. My boss is sick and he needs me to give a presentation in the morning."

"Are we still shearing tonight?" asked Tony.

"We're still shearing," said his father. "It's just that I need a haircut for tomorrow. Boy, I hope the barber opens early. I can't give a presentation looking like this! Now let's start on those sheep!"

When they sheared the sheep, it was Tony's job to get each animal ready. His father held them and gently ran the shears along their skin. Shearing took real skill. The shears cut just as fine as barber's clippers. But as with any clippers, it was still possible to cut the skin if one wasn't careful. At the livestock fair, other people always commented on how skilled Tony's father was. Once he flicked the shears on, it was no time at all before the sheep were stripped of their wool, and had barely a nick on them.

Together they sheared till late that night. Finally, there was only one more sheep left. They had filled ten large bags with wool, and a herd of pink-skinned sheep stood shivering slightly in a nearby pen.

"I'm going to let you finish this last one," said his father, handing Tony the shears.

"Really?" asked Tony in surprise. He had always wanted to, but he had never tried before. He had watched his dad many times. He turned the shears on. A slight vibration spread through his hand. He started slowly trying to gently capture the wool in long strips, like his father always did. It took him a long time. When he was finished he looked up. Bits of wool stuck in his father's hair.

"You did a great job, Tony," said his father. "Now, let's take those shears inside and find a comb and a pair of scissors. I need you to give me a haircut."

"What?" said Tony, in amazement. "Dad, I can't."

"Don't worry!" his dad reassured him. "If you can't get my hair completely even, that's okay. It's just my city job!"

# Dad's Haircut *(cont.)*

**After reading the story, answer the questions.  Circle the correct answer.**

1. How did Tony learn to shear sheep?
   a. By watching his father and then doing it himself
   b. By giving his father a haircut
   c. By going to the livestock fair
   d. By shearing the sheep when his father was busy at work

2. Tony's father was known as—
   a. a "weekend farmer"
   b. a "hard worker"
   c. "curly head"
   d. a "sheep shearer"

3. The reader can tell from this story that—
   a. Tony's father is more concerned with hard work than appearances
   b. Tony and his father should spend more time together
   c. Tony felt very confident when he sheared his first sheep
   d. other people view Tony's father as a skilled presenter

4. The passage gives one reason to believe that Tony depended on his father for everything except—
   a. oiling the shears
   b. shearing the sheep
   c. deciding when to shear the sheep
   d. holding onto the sheep

5. Which of the following can you conclude from this story?
   a. People at the livestock fair will know which sheep Tony sheared.
   b. Tony will probably not be allowed to shear sheep again.
   c. Tony will probably shear more sheep in the future.
   d. Tony's father will probably quit his job in the city.

6. The web shows some ideas discussed in the article.  Which of these belongs in the empty box?
   a. pink-skinned sheep
   b. feeds the sheep
   c. oils the shears
   d. big, curly hair

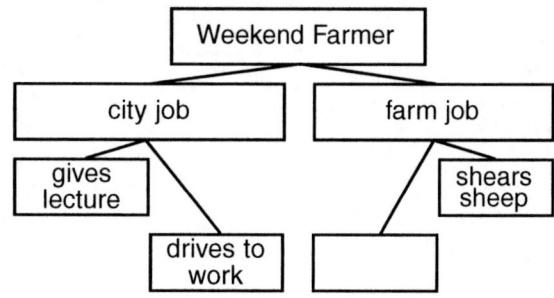

# Grandpa's Plane

Grandpa showed the newspaper picture to Ursula. "This plane is on tour, and it's coming to town this weekend. Would you like to go with me on Saturday to see it?" he asked. Ursula looked at the picture of the B-17 bomber that he had shown her. She looked back up at her grandfather. She didn't see him get this excited very often.

"Okay, Grandpa, I'll go," she said, with a smile.

On their way out to see the plane that Saturday, Grandpa told Ursula all about his experiences during the war. He told her about how he had been stationed in England during the early years of World War II. He had piloted one of those B-17s and had flown missions 200 miles into Germany. He told her that the planes back then weren't pressurized or heated. There were big openings on the sides for the gun operators, so it was very cold when they were in the air. The crew had to wear heavy flight suits that were lined with sheepskin. These missions were also very dangerous because German anti-aircraft guns on the ground would do everything they could to knock the American planes out of the air. The anti-aircraft fire would often pound the air around the planes for the entire time they were over Germany. It would not stop until they were over the North Sea again and on their way home.

When Ursula and her grandpa got out of the car, they saw the plane immediately. The bright sun reflected off the round body of the B-17 and the broad surfaces of its wings. Glass covered the nose, and long gun barrels pointed out at sharp angles from holes in the body.

The plane was impressive, Ursula thought, but it was not very large. She had seen jumbo jets and big cargo planes at airports in the past. She couldn't imagine how this craft, one-third the size of a 747, could have carried all those bombs and flown so far. It looked dangerous just to get inside it.

After walking around the plane once, Ursula walked over to a short ladder that led into the belly of the craft. Once inside, she had to stoop over so she wouldn't hit her head. After Grandpa had pulled himself into the plane behind her, the two of them climbed up into the pilot's and co-pilot's seats. Grandpa showed Ursula the instruments, one at a time. She saw the airspeed indicator, the vertical speed indicator, and the artificial horizon. Grandpa explained that there had to be two gauges, one on each side of the cockpit, so that both the pilot and co-pilot could fly the plane if necessary.

"The planes were pretty simple compared to today's planes," Grandpa explained. "There were no computers or radar. They were amazingly tough, though. Even though my plane often got beat up by the anti-aircraft fire, it brought me home every time."

When they got back to the car, Ursula gave her grandpa a big hug. He looked at her and asked, "What was that for?"

"For showing me part of your life, Grandpa. Your stories make more sense to me now. I understand a little more what it was like for you in the war so long ago."

*Fiction*

# Grandpa' Plane *(cont.)*

**After reading the story, answer the questions.  Circle the correct answer.**

1. Why did Ursula and her grandpa go to see the B-17 bomber?
    a. Ursula's grandpa had always wanted to see one.
    b. Ursula was learning about the war in school.
    c. Ursula was very interested in old warplanes.
    d. Ursula's grandpa flew a B-17 in World War II.

2. When did the B-17 crew wear heavy flight suits?
    a. Whenever they flew the B-17's
    b. When they were told to dress in uniform
    c. During the wintertime
    d. When they needed protection from crashing

3. The reason planes were simple in the 1940s is that—
    a. much of the equipment on planes today is due to advances in technology since the 1940s
    b. pilots did not have time to be trained on special equipment
    c. planes made for wartime were always basic and simple because so many needed to be built
    d. they needed to stay as light as possible so they had no special equipment

4. The reader can tell from the story that Ursula's grandpa—
    a. wished he hadn't taken Ursula to see the B-17
    b. was happy to see the B-17
    c. was sad to see the B-17
    d. did not care about seeing the B-17

5. Which of the following is an opinion in this story?
    a. "These missions were also very dangerous."
    b. "There had to be two gauges, one on each side of the cockpit."
    c. "It looked dangerous just to get inside it."
    d. "She had to stoop over so she wouldn't hit her head."

6. Information in the story suggests that—
    a. Ursula will become a pilot like her grandfather when she grows up
    b. Ursula's interest in B-17 bombers started before Grandpa took her on a tour
    c. Grandpa's war stories were confusing to Ursula before touring the B-17 bomber
    d. Grandpa will take Ursula's younger brother to see a B-17 bomber soon

# The Rock Hound

Tashi was walking on the beach looking for stones for his collection. Most people at the ocean walked down to where the water washed strange and beautiful things onto the beach. Then they picked up the shells or wood or other odd things they happened to find. Not Tashi. Tashi wasn't interested in shells. Tashi was a rock hound, someone who collects unusual stones. He had a big collection of the rocks he had found. He labeled each one to tell what it was and where it came from.

Near the beach was a cliff that was a perfect place to hunt rocks. The face of the cliff went straight up about fifty feet. When it rained, stones and soil washed down the cliff face and gathered at the bottom. After a strong rainstorm, Tashi would hunt for unusual rocks there. He had a plastic pail he used to collect his finds. He used a field guide about rocks and minerals to figure out what each rock was. The field guide fit in his pocket so he could easily carry it. It had pictures of many different kinds of rocks and their crystal shapes. Rocks look like they are solid, but most are really made of thousands of grains of sand or of crystals. Different rocks have different crystal shapes. Tashi used a magnifying glass to look at the grains and crystals in each rock to see their shape. That way he could tell what each rock was.

Tashi looked down and saw a bright black stone about the size of an apple. It was cracked in half. He picked it up and looked at it. It was shiny, like stones called agates that he often found on the beach. But agates are usually orange or red. This stone was totally black. Agates also have layers or "bands" on them. Tashi looked closely at the new stone with his magnifying glass. He tried to see if the stone had crystals or grains inside it. The stone was completely solid. It didn't have any crystals or grains at all. The inside looked just like a piece of black glass. Tashi didn't know what it was, so he checked his book.

Because the stone was shiny like an agate, he looked at stones in the agate "family." None matched his new find. Then Tashi looked at a chart in the book that listed rocks by their crystal type. The chart listed a type of rock with no crystals or grains. It was called "obsidian." Tashi looked that up in his field book. The book said that obsidian is a glasslike, shiny rock without crystals that forms when volcanoes explode. It is often black. "That must be it!" thought Tashi. He knew obsidian was very rare where he lived. He had never found any before and was very excited. To be sure it didn't get scratched, he put the rock in his pocket instead of in the pail with the other stones. Obsidian isn't worth any money, but for a rock hound like Tashi, finding a rare stone like that was as exciting as finding gold.

# The Rock Hound *(cont.)*

**After reading the story, answer the questions. Circle the correct answer.**

1. The reason Tashi put the black rock in his pocket is—
   a. he liked how shiny and black the rock was
   b. he didn't want it to get scratched
   c. he knew it was very valuable
   d. he knew obsidian was hard to find anywhere

2. According to this story a good place to find rocks is—
   a. in the ocean
   b. on a beach
   c. in the desert
   d. at the bottom of a cliff

3. Tashi probably used a field guide—
   a. to help identify the rocks
   b. because he liked looking at the rock pictures
   c. to look closely at the grains and crystals in each rock
   d. to help find the rocks

4. According to the story, the black rock is rare where Tashi lives because—
   a. there are probably no active volcanoes where Tashi lives
   b. the rock is rare everywhere
   c. there are no bodies of water where Tashi lives
   d. there are no mountains where Tashi lives

5. Which of the following is an opinion?
   a. Most people like shells better than rocks.
   b. Obsidian rock comes from volcanoes.
   c. Different rocks have different crystal shapes.
   d. Tashi was interested in shells.

6. You could probably find this story in a book about—
   a. beach combing
   b. shells and driftwood
   c. trees and plants
   d. rock collecting experiences

# The Perfect Picture

Jo and Kerry were friends who lived in a big city. One day Kerry's dad asked her if she would like to go camping out in the woods.

"I sure would!" Kerry exclaimed happily. "Can Jo come with us?" she continued.

Kerry's dad answered, "As long as it is okay with her parents."

Kerry ran over to Jo's house as fast as she could and knocked on the door. Jo's mom opened it.

"Hello, Kerry. Need a glass of water?"

Kerry's face was red, and she was breathing loudly. "No thanks," gasped Kerry. "I came to see Jo."

"She's up in her room. You know the way," replied Jo's mom.

Kerry rushed down the long hallway and then climbed the 15 stairs to the second floor. Jo's room was the third door on the left, and Kerry knocked on it. When Jo opened the door, Kerry blurted out, "Guess what? My dad is taking me camping!"

"You are so lucky," said Jo. "I wish I could go camping."

"Well," said Kerry, "your wish has come true. Dad says you may come if your parents say it's okay."

Jo let out a small shriek and ran out the door. "Mom!" she called. "Can I please go camping with Kerry and her dad?"

"Of course," Jo's mom replied.

"Great!" shouted the girls together.

The next day, Kerry's dad drove high into the mountains. When they reached their campsite, he showed Kerry and Jo how to set up the tent. Then he took them on a hike. Kerry made sure to bring her camera. Before they started, Kerry's dad said, "There are two rules. One, you must stick close to me on the trail. No running off on your own. Two, you each must find something special; something you can't get in the city."

The first thing they saw was a deer track. Jo remembered seeing tracks like these in the park near her house. "Not special enough," said Jo.

Kerry's dad smiled, and they continued hiking. A little while later, Jo found a feather on the ground. Kerry's dad said the feather had belonged to a golden eagle.

"We don't see those in the city," commented Jo.

Kerry looked all around for something special, too, but she could not find anything. A short while later, the three sat down on a big rock to enjoy their lunches.

"Time to head back," Kerry's dad said, when he noticed they had all finished.

All the way back to camp, Kerry looked for something special. She saw pine trees and songbirds and pebbles along the trail, but she did not think any of those were special enough. Rocks are everywhere, she thought, and we have trees and songbirds at home. Finally they reached camp.

"Well, Kerry, what did you find?" asked her dad.

Kerry looked around the camp. She saw their sleeping bags rolled out in the tent and the stove set up on a stump. She looked at her dad and smiled. "I found this beautiful picture." With that, she held up her camera and took a picture of her dad and her best friend smiling in front of the tent.

# The Perfect Picture (cont.)

**After reading the story, answer the questions. Circle the correct answer.**

1. This story is mostly about
   a. a picnic lunch in the forest
   b. finding something special
   c. friends in the city
   d. buying a camera

2. Which of these best describes Jo's feelings when her mother gave her permission to go camping?
   a. Jo was afraid she would get lost in the woods.
   b. Jo was excited about going camping.
   c. Jo was wishing her mother had said no.
   d. Jo was excited about using her camera.

3. Your answer choice for Number 2 is best supported by which of these ideas from the story?
   a. Jo stayed close to Kerry and her dad so she would not get lost.
   b. Jo learned how to set up the tent at their campsite.
   c. Jo wanted to go camping and exclaimed it was great when her mother gave her permission.
   d. Jo said that the deer tracks were not special enough.

4. Which of these actions caused Kerry to hold up her camera?
   a. Kerry saw a beautiful golden eagle flying overhead.
   b. Kerry saw a perfect picture at the end of the hike.
   c. Kerry wanted Jo to have something special to take home.
   d. Kerry wanted her dad to take a picture of her and Jo.

5. Jo decided the eagle feather was special because
   a. it was something she could not find in the city
   b. she thought it was a good luck charm
   c. it would remind her of a special bird
   d. she would beat Kerry in the contest

6. According to the passage, Kerry saw "the stove set up on a stump." Used this way the word "stump" probably means
   a. to confuse or perplex
   b. to walk clumsily
   c. the lower end of a tree trunk
   d. part of a tooth

# Lester's Find

Lester liked to collect things. He would walk down the sidewalk near his apartment building with his eyes focused on the ground. He was always hoping that something interesting would present itself at his feet. Lester had found many things this way. He had found a used spark plug, a soda bottle with foreign lettering on it, and his real prize—a plastic doll from his favorite cartoon show. Whenever he found an object that interested him, he added it to the collection on his dresser. He called them his "odds and ends."

One day, Lester was walking home from school. As usual, he had his eyes glued to the pavement, hoping for something to add to his collection. Just as he turned the corner to his street, Lester glimpsed something on the ground at the very edge of the curb. When he bent down to pick it up, he was amazed! It was small, but it was very shiny and sparkled in the sun. It was a tiny rock, carved into a round pyramid shape. "It's a diamond!" he thought. He could not be sure, though. He had never really seen any diamonds except for the one in his mother's ring.

Lester picked the rock up and carefully put it into his pocket. When he reached his house, he ran to his bedroom, dropped his books on the bed, and went to his desk near the window, where there was more light. He pulled a magnifying glass out of the drawer and began to examine his find. It looked like a diamond. Then Lester remembered something. He had heard that diamonds can cut glass, so he took the rock into the bathroom. He held it up to the very bottom corner of the mirror where nobody would notice a scratch, and he rubbed the rock on the mirror. It grated a little, and when Lester pulled it away, there was a tiny cut in the mirror's surface. It was a real diamond!

"It must have fallen out of someone's ring," Lester thought. Then he began to frown. "That means somebody lost it. I know I would be very sad to lose something so beautiful." He thought about what his mom had said about finding something valuable. "You should always give it to the police, so they can try to find the owner," she had told him.

When Lester's mom came home from work, he showed her the stone and asked what he should do with it. "We can go down to the police station after I get home tomorrow," she replied. "You did the right thing by showing me this. I know that if I had lost the diamond out of my ring, I would be very upset."

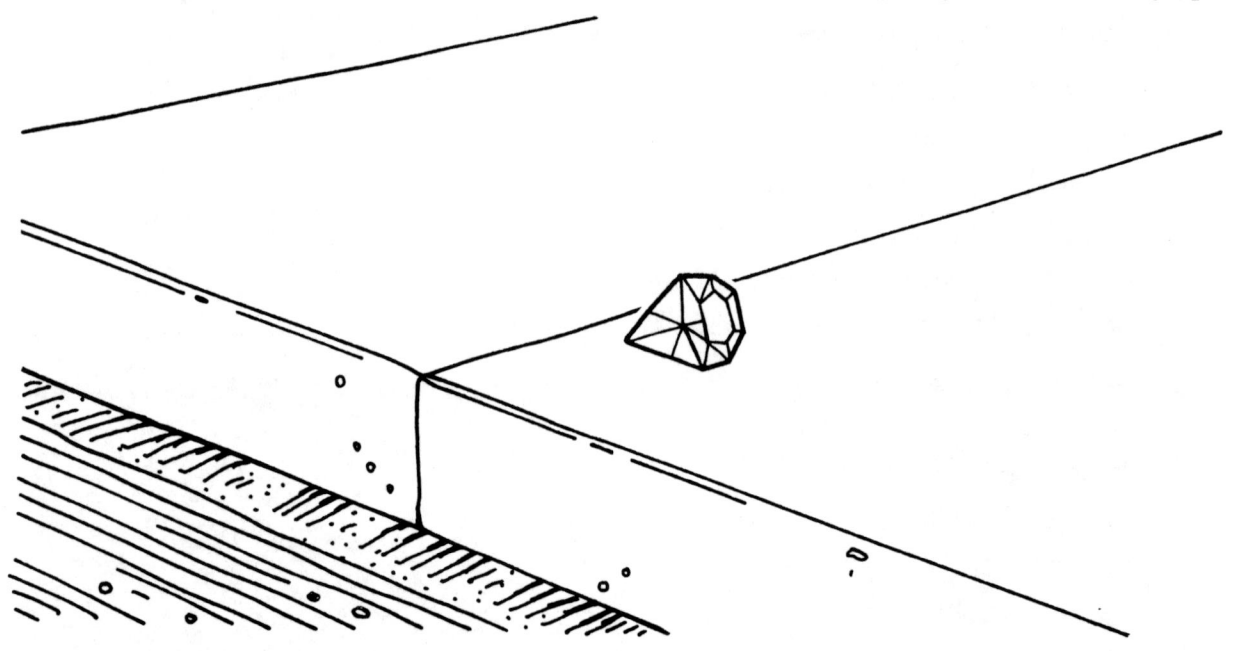

# Lester's Find *(cont.)*

The next day, Lester carried the tiny stone in his hand up to the front counter in the police station. Lester told the policeman behind the counter where he had found the rock and how he thought it might be valuable. "Thank you, young man," the policeman said. "I'm glad you brought this to me." They went over to a desk, and with his mom's help, Lester started to fill out the police forms.

When they were done, the policeman shook Lester's hand. "Thanks again, Lester. You did the right thing coming down here today," he said. "By the way, did I mention that if no one claims this diamond within six months, there is a good chance that you will be able to keep it?"

Lester looked up at his mom. "Is that true?" he asked her.

"Yes, Lester. If no one claims the diamond, the police are allowed to let you keep it under a law called 'the found-property law.' If you had not brought the diamond to the police and just kept it, you might have been breaking the law. Since you did bring it to the police, there is a chance you could get to keep it legally."

Lester walked out of the police station with a big grin on his face. He was glad he had given the diamond to the police, and he thought about how happy it would make someone to get it back. Still, Lester hoped that maybe he would get to keep his diamond.

# Lester's Find *(cont.)*

**After reading the story, answer the questions.  Circle the correct answer.**

1. This passage is mostly about
    a. how to determine what diamonds cost
    b. the different things that Lester collects
    c. how to identify different rocks
    d. the unusual treasure Lester found

2. After Lester brought the diamond home, he began to "examine" it.  Which of these words means the same as examine?
    a. scratch
    b. question
    c. inspect
    d. rub

3. If no one claims the diamond within six months, how will the police know who to give it to?
    a. The forms that Lester filled out have his name on them.
    b. The diamond matches the one in Lester's mother's ring.
    c. The law says the police get to keep the diamond.
    d. The police will place an ad looking for the owner.

4. By the end of the passage, Lester's feelings have changed from
    a. excitement to fear
    b. sympathy to contentment
    c. happiness to anger
    d. curiosity to confusion

5. The advice of Lester's mother is most like a
    a. coach telling a team to play fair
    b. teacher telling a class to clear their desks
    c. doctor telling a patient to say "Aaah"
    d. sergeant telling a group of soldiers to march

6. Lester hopes that no one claims the diamond because
    a. he'd like to keep it
    b. his mother wants to put it in her ring
    c. he wants to give it to the owner himself
    d. he doesn't want to make the owner happy about having gotten it back

# Keyboard Master:  Mozart

Wolfgang Amadeus Mozart is one of the world's most famous musicians.  As an adult, he produced more than 600 works, including symphonies, operas, and other musical pieces.  What is most unusual about Mozart is that he amazed the world with his musical brilliance when he was only six years old.

Mozart was born in Austria in 1756.  It wasn't long before his father noticed Mozart's talent for music.  The small boy would listen to his sister Nannerl's music lessons, then try to play along.  Mozart learned an entire piece of music by heart when he was only four years old.

Both Mozart and Nannerl came from a very talented family.  Their father, Leopold, was a violinist and composer.  Their mother, Anna Maria, came from a family of musicians.

Leopold wanted the world to see what brilliant children Mozart and Nannerl were.  When Mozart was six and Nannerl was ten, Leopold took them on a European tour.  The family traveled for four years.  They went to Austria, Hungary, Germany, France, England, the Netherlands, and Switzerland.  Everywhere they went, the children charmed audiences with their musical abilities.

Sometimes Mozart and Nannerl would play duets.  Their fingers flew over the keys in a blur.  Sometimes Leopold asked Mozart to do musical "tricks."  One of Mozart's favorite tricks was to play the harpsichord with a cloth draped over the keys so he couldn't see them.  For another trick, Mozart would listen through a door while someone played music he had never heard.  Then the boy would enter the room and play the piece perfectly.

After the tour, the family went back home to Austria.  But Mozart and Leopold couldn't stay still for long.  Soon they went on another tour, then another.  By the time Mozart was sixteen, he was one of the best known musicians in Europe.  Royalty asked him to compose operas just for them.

As he grew up, people were not quite as amazed at Mozart's talent as they were when he was a child.  Mozart made a living by composing music, giving concerts, and teaching, but his music eventually fell out of favor with the people of his time.  He died at the age of 35, deeply in debt.

Today, Mozart is recognized as one of the greatest musicians that the world has ever known, and his music and operas are even more popular than when he was alive.

# Keyboard Master: Mozart

**After reading the story, answer the questions. Circle the correct answer.**

1. Why did Mozart's father take his children on a European tour?
   a. He wanted to make a living through his children's talents.
   b. He wanted his children to see all of Europe.
   c. He wanted to expand their musical abilities.
   d. He wanted the world to see what brilliant children they were.

2. How old was Mozart when he played his first musical piece by heart?
   a. Six
   b. Sixteen
   c. Four
   d. Ten

3. What does the passage mean by "the children charmed audiences"?
   a. The audiences would be amazed and awed by the children's talents.
   b. The people in the audience would fall asleep.
   c. The children would give small musical charms to the people in the audience.
   d. The children were always polite and well behaved.

4. According to the passage—
   a. Mozart died a happy man.
   b. Mozart became more popular as an adult musician.
   c. Mozart's popularity decreased as he got older.
   d. Mozart's operas are less popular now than when he was alive.

5. Which of the following can you conclude from this passage?
   a. Mozart died not knowing that his music would live on.
   b. There has never been a musician as talented as Mozart.
   c. Music changed dramatically after Mozart's death.
   d. Mozart knew he would be remembered as a world famous musician.

6. The web shows some important ideas in the story. Which of these belongs in the empty box?
   a. cloth drape
   b. violinist and composer
   c. musical tricks
   d. deep in debt

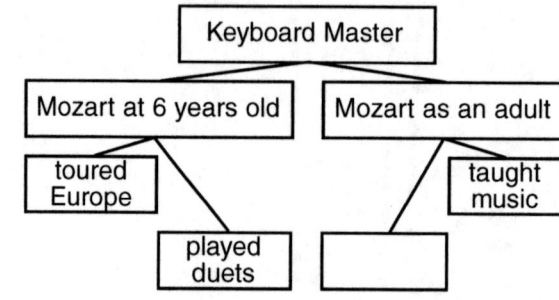

# Birth of an Island

Islands aren't born very often. Sometimes islands are created when a volcano erupts below the surface of the ocean. The lava cools and builds the volcano up. When the volcano gets tall enough, it pokes through the surface of the ocean. In the Atlantic Ocean, both Iceland and the Canary Islands were formed this way. Some islands, like Hawaii in the Pacific Ocean, are still being formed!

In 1963, a crew on a fishing boat was present when one island was being born. Early one morning the boat was sailing near the coast of Iceland. The crew awoke to what smelled like rotten eggs. No one knew what the source of the smell was. Suddenly, the boat began rocking back and forth. The sea began to boil like a pot of dark stew. Smoke started to rise out of the water. An underwater volcano was erupting right in front of their eyes!

The captain and his crew moved the vessel and watched from a distance. The volcano spit rock and lava into the air. It looked like the sky was raining rocks. The volcano erupted for days. Finally the fires burned themselves out. The top of the volcano was sticking up out of the ocean. When the lava on top of the volcano cooled, a new island sat where only water had been before.

Scientists were very excited because they had never seen a brand-new island. The scientists named the new island Surtsey, after the Icelandic god of fire. It was the perfect name for such a fiery island.

But the new island did not look much like other islands. It was only a pile of bare rock. There were no plants or animals on it. Scientists wondered how life would come to an empty island. They set up camp and watched and waited. Finally, after many months, a single plant began growing on the rocks. Scientists found that birds would often land on the island and drop plant materials that had been trapped in their feathers and claws. Sometimes, the birds would drop seeds and a plant would begin to grow.

Today, there are a lot of birds and plants living on Surtsey. Humans are not allowed to go there except for a few scientists. The island is protected so that it can be studied. Surtsey is the perfect place to learn how plants and animals spread to new places around the earth.

# Birth of an Island (cont.)

**After reading the story, answer the questions.  Circle the correct answer.**

1. The author compares the sea to—
   a. a pot of stew
   b. raining rocks
   c. the god of fire
   d. rotten eggs

2. How was Surtsey formed?
   a. A volcano erupted below the surface of the ocean.
   b. Birds would drop plant material in the same spot.
   c. The sky rained rocks until it was formed.
   d. The Icelandic god of fire created it.

3. Studying Surtsey is important because—
   a. underwater volcanoes have never erupted before
   b. it teaches scientists how plants and animals spread to new places
   c. humans are not allowed to go there
   d. scientists had never studied volcanoes before

4. Which of these best describes the scientists' feelings when they first visited the new island of Surtsey?
   a. scared
   b. confident
   c. excited
   d. upset

5. Which of these sentences best explains what scientists think about Surtsey?
   a. The captain and his crew moved the vessel and watched from a distance.
   b. Today, there are a lot of birds and plants living on Surtsey.
   c. Surtsey is a rare opportunity to study what had never been studied before.
   d. It was the perfect name for such a fiery island.

6. What is the probable reason the new island was named after a god of fire?
   a. The island has many forest fires.
   b. The island was a pile of bare rocks.
   c. The island was made by a volcano.
   d. The island is really hot in the summer.

# Grizzlies

Grizzly bears are among the largest bears in the world. They are observed and studied by wildlife biologists in order to keep the grizzly population from becoming extinct.

These big bears are usually found in Alaska, where they are called "brown bears" or sometimes "brownies." Biologists locate bears by their tracks—footprints with claws far forward of the footpad. Other telltale signs of grizzlies are high claw marks on trees.

These bears usually stake out their favorite fishing holes, either in a stream or right below a waterfall. To watch a grizzly catch a fish is amazing. The bear will stand on the edge of the falls and hang its head out. Sometimes the bear will grab a fish in midair. A grizzly can eat up to a hundred pounds of salmon in a day.

Grizzlies can be dangerous, so it is important to know what to do if you see one. One hiker saved a friend from a grizzly attack when she opened her umbrella in the bear's face as it charged. When a bear rears up, lays its ears back, makes a "woofing" sound several times or a popping sound with its jaws, look out! If you turn and run, the bear will probably attack.

Instead, your best defense against an angry grizzly is to make yourself look as big as possible without making any threatening gestures. Do not look the bear in the eye. Talk softly and apologetically. If the bear still charges, it will probably stop before it gets to you. Or, it may run right past you.

These bears can be fun to watch from a distance. One man saw a group of bears slide down the same snow bank two or three times in a row. In Montana, the same observer saw a grizzly sit down and watch an especially beautiful sunset. The bear watched for twenty minutes. As soon as the sun had set, the grizzly got up and left.

# Grizzlies *(cont.)*

**After reading the story, answer the questions.  Circle the correct answer.**

1. Why is it important to know what to do if you see a grizzly?

    a. Grizzlies travel in groups, so where there is one there are probably several.

    b. Grizzlies may become extinct so you need to remember where you saw one.

    c. Grizzlies can be dangerous and might attack.

    d. Grizzlies always feel threatened by humans.

2. When a grizzly is angry it—

    a. crouches low to the ground

    b. lays its ears back

    c. makes a hissing sound

    d. spits at the intruder

3. What is the main idea of the last paragraph?

    a. Grizzlies are often shy.

    b. Grizzlies can be dangerous.

    c. Grizzlies are very scary.

    d. Grizzlies can be funny.

4. In order to keep a grizzly from attacking, the author suggests—

    a. talking quietly and not making eye contact

    b. throwing something at the grizzly's face

    c. crouching down and covering your head

    d. jumping up and down

5. Information in this passage suggests that grizzlies—

    a. are smaller than many bears

    b. should be allowed to become extinct

    c. are not very fond of fish

    d. often become attached to certain spots

6. This passage can best be described as—

    a. nonfiction

    b. historical

    c. a short story

    d. a tall tale

# For the Record

Thomas Edison made the first sound recording in 1877. He recorded himself singing "Mary Had a Little Lamb." At the time, people did not think Edison's invention would be useful. Many people laughed at him. At the time, his recording machine seemed unbelievable. Until that day, the only way to hear music was to be near a musician. People couldn't believe that sound could be saved! One scientist even claimed that Edison had faked the sound.

Edison's recording machine was called the phonograph. It was difficult to use. To record sound, someone had to turn a crank exactly sixty times a minute. When the recording was played back, someone had to again turn the crank at exactly the same speed, or the recording wouldn't sound right.

The early recordings did not look like the ones we see today. They were cylinders covered with tinfoil. The phonograph had a needle that scratched the sound into the tinfoil. This was a complex process. The recordings were not very clear. They could only be played back a few times before the foil tore or wore out. People generally did not like making recordings because of the hard work involved.

Ten years later, inventor Emile Berliner designed a better recording machine. It used a flat disc, which he called a record. These discs were made of plastic. They lasted a lot longer than the tinfoil cylinders. He also invented a way to make copies of a recording. Berliner's improvements were important. The record disc brought music into everyone's homes. For the first time, one could buy music and play it over and over on a player at home.

It took a long time before records became practical. Berliner's records only held about two minutes of music. In 1948, Columbia Records introduced the long-playing record, or LP. It held up to 30 minutes of music per side. Much more music could fit on an LP. Long symphonies could now be recorded. The LP changed music recording all over the world.

The LP came at the perfect time. In the 1950s, popular music and culture were growing very quickly. It was the time of rock and roll. Many new musicians wanted to make recordings, and many young people wanted to buy them. The LP made it possible for radio stations to play different kinds of music. Also, people could share their favorite music with each other.

In the 1960s, people could also buy music on magnetic tapes. These tapes were eventually put into plastic cases called cassettes. Cassettes were very popular. They were inexpensive and much more portable than LPs. In 1979, Sony invented the Walkman. It played cassettes and had headphones that the user could wear anywhere. The Walkman allowed people to listen to music even if they were jogging in the park or reading in the library.

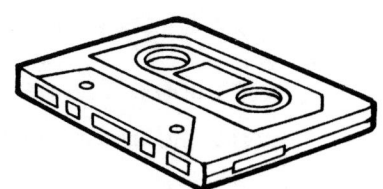

Three years later, CDs, or compact discs, were introduced. They sounded much better than any type of recording had before. CDs could also hold over an hour of music. By the early 1990s, CDs had mostly replaced LPs.

Sound recording is still being improved. Music fans can now find music on the Internet. They can also save music on memory chips that are portable like a Walkman.

In 1877, people laughed at Edison's first scratchy recording of "Mary Had a Little Lamb." But what he started over a hundred years ago was the beginning of an important change in the way people share sounds and music.

# For the Record *(cont.)*

**After reading the story, answer the questions.  Circle the correct answer.**

1. Which of these happened last in the passage?
   a. Sony invented the Walkman.
   b. Compact discs were introduced.
   c. People bought music on magnetic tapes.
   d. Columbia Records introduced the LP.

2. Thomas Edison's recording machine was called a—
   a. long-playing record
   b. phonograph
   c. cassette
   d. photograph

3. Why was Emile Berliner's record disc an important improvement in sound recording?
   a. It held over an hour of music.
   b. It allowed people to easily play music at home.
   c. It was inexpensive and portable.
   d. It evolved during the time of rock and roll.

4. Which is the main idea of this passage?
   a. It took a long time before records became practical.
   b. Sound recording technology has gone through many changes and improvements since its invention.
   c. Thomas Edison invented the first sound recording.
   d. Early recordings were difficult to hear and did not last long.

5. Information in this passage suggests that—
   a. people in the late 1800s valued the achievements of inventors
   b. people in the late 1800s predicted Thomas Edison would be famous
   c. Thomas Edison's early music invention started an entire industry
   d. Thomas Edison's invention was popular to use at social events

6. A good addition near the end of the passage might be a paragraph about—
   a. Thomas Edison
   b. ways that people entertain themselves
   c. compact discs
   d. Sony and its Walkman invention

# Building a Medieval Castle

In the Middle Ages, kings fought one another to gain control of land. When a king won a victory, he sometimes granted lands to his favorite knights. The only catch was that the knight had to protect the lands from invaders. To do that, a sturdy castle had to be built. The castle protected the knight, his army of men and their weapons, and it was a place of safety for the townspeople. A mighty castle also showed everyone how powerful the knight was.

Building a castle was a long, messy job. During the Middle Ages, there were no power tools. Workers did not use steel or iron to build strong castle walls. There were no bulldozers or steam shovels. All of the work was done with wooden tools, pulleys, and muscle.

First, a special castle architect drew up plans for the castle. Did the knight want four towers or ten? Should the towers be round or square? Would there be big, open rooms or small chambers? When the knight liked what he saw, the plans were finished.

Then a call went out to all of the people in the land. Laborers from surrounding villages came to the construction site looking for work. There were masons (brick layers), stone cutters, carpenters, blacksmiths, and diggers. A worker lucky enough to be hired knew he would have a job for as long as ten years! That's the length of time it could take to build one castle.

Building was usually undertaken from April to November. Even during those months, work got done only during good weather. A long rainy season could mean a whole year's work was lost. When the work was going on, there could be more than 2,000 workers living, eating, and sleeping at the site.

Building a castle cost a lot of money, too. Feeding, housing, and paying all of the workers, plus the cost of construction materials, added up. One castle might cost many millions of dollars in today's money.

# Building a Medieval Castle *(cont.)*

**After reading the story, answer the questions.  Circle the correct answer.**

1. Why might workers move their families close to a newly built castle?
   a. to be near a knight
   b. to have a job in the future
   c. to be safe
   d. to gain control of the land

2. The author of the passage would probably agree that
   a. knights did not deserve to live in a castle
   b. castles were a lot of work and cost a lot of money
   c. castle building was a swift process
   d. townspeople did not benefit from a castle

3. The author probably wrote this passage to
   a. describe how a castle was built
   b. show how weather affected castle building
   c. explain the job of a castle architect
   d. list the kinds of occupations workers had

4. When the passage says that there was a catch when the king gave a knight some land, it means that
   a. there was a hidden problem
   b. the knight had to trap the animals on the land
   c. there was no house to live in
   d. the knight had to design the castle himself

5. The architect's responsibility included
   a. finding workers to build the castle
   b. determining how long it would take to build the castle
   c. designing and drawing up plans for the castle
   d. getting the money

6. A mason's job would have been to
   a. cut wood
   b. dig ditches
   c. find stones
   d. lay bricks

# David Scott-Risner: Art is a Calling

David Scott-Risner's office is a little cottage that used to be an art studio, somewhat hidden away in the woods. He is an artist and a designer who works for Cornish College of the Arts in Seattle, Washington. He helped design the remodeling of some of the college's buildings. He is very curious and interested in people. He calls himself an optimist, which means he has a positive outlook on life. David also believes in serendipity, which is a kind of luck. Here is an interview with him.

**Do you like your job at Cornish College?**

This is something I find creative.

**Where did you go to school?**

I studied sculpture at Cranbrook Art Academy. Then I worked and studied with architect James Hubbell.

**How did you meet Mr. Hubbell?**

He had gone to Cranbook Art Academy, too, before I did.

**An architect designs buildings. A sculptor carves or designs art out of wood, bronze, marble, or stone. Are you an architect or a sculptor?**

I think I work a lot differently from most architects. I had two compelling forces in my life, architecture and sculpture. I try to use the skills I learned from both. It seems to work well for me.

**Are you saying that you use both art and architecture in your work?**

Yes. I feel that we must incorporate art into everything we do, all the time. There is no difference between making a living and making art, even if your paintings (or dances or music) are not selling. Your art cannot be separated from you. My friend Molly is a choreographer, someone who makes dances. She uses the same skills for her art as she does to relate to the people around her every day.

**Do you work with other types of artists?**

In 1993, two friends and I opened the Mask gallery in Detroit. My friend Hava Jean Delgado is a choreographer, and my friend Eugene Clark is an artist-musician. We wanted the Mask gallery to be a place where artists of all kinds could display or perform their work.

**Who inspires you? Who do you look up to?**

Architect Frank Lloyd Wright. He designed many types of buildings. He believed that form follows function, that something beautiful must also be useful. He wrote a great book called *The Natural House*. Years later I'm still inspired by what he did. Architect and designer Antonio Gaudi influenced me as well. James Hubbell, the architect I studied with when I got out of school, uses many of the same ideas that Gaudi used, like curving lines.

**Gaudi also liked to use natural materials in his buildings. Do you?**

Yes. I like to use organic materials, things not made by humans. Also, I am more interested in how we create or make things. The way we create is more important to me than the creation itself. This applies to art, architecture, and everything.

**How did you become interested in art and architecture?**

I believe that art is a calling. It is something our insides tell us we must do. Some people must make dances. Some people must make buildings. Sometimes it is serendipity, or luck, that brings us to our work. I was lucky to find two things I love—art and architecture.

# David Scott-Risner: Art is a Calling *(cont.)*

**After reading the story, answer the questions. Circle the correct answer.**

1. The interview you have just read is mostly about
   a. what it is like to be an architect
   b. how a young man learned sculpture
   c. ways that different artists interact
   d. ways that work and life are connected

2. What important lesson did Scott-Risner learn from architect Frank Lloyd Wright?
   a. something beautiful must also be useful
   b. a good architect should make natural houses
   c. how to make many different kinds of buildings
   d. how to write architectural books

3. When Scott-Risner says that his art cannot be separated from him, he probably means that
   a. his artwork cannot be given away
   b. once you learn art, you cannot forget it
   c. art is a basic part of his personality
   d. he is worried his art might be stolen

4. According to the interview, Scott-Risner has had two _____ in his life. Choose the word that means compelling forces.
   a. influences
   b. obstacles
   c. regrets
   d. opinions

5. What did Scott-Risner say was more important than the work of art itself?
   a. the use of organic materials in art
   b. the way to display or perform art
   c. the way art is created
   d. the use of curved lines in art

6. This interview with Scott-Risner could be used to answer which of the following questions?
   a. How can a person know if he should be creating art?
   b. What are the best schools for studying art?
   c. Where are the best places for artists to live?
   d. How many years does it take to become an artist?

# Native American Games and Sports

Renaud recently joined the school lacrosse team.  Lacrosse is a fast-paced game in which two teams of players use long rackets with a net on the end to pass a ball while running up and down a field.  Renaud's coach told him that the game was originally played by Native Americans and that some tribes, like the Iroquois, still compete in international lacrosse competitions.  Renaud was intrigued by this and did more research on Native American games.  He compiled a list of these games to share with his lacrosse teammates, along with the following message.

**Greetings Lacrosse Players!**

I thought everyone would enjoy learning about a few more games originally played by the tribes of North America.  Some of these games will seem familiar to you because they are played much like games we already know.  Gather a group of friends and play one of these games!

*Renaud*

| Game | Description | Tribe |
|---|---|---|
| Double ball | A game similar to lacrosse, but only women were allowed to play. | Northeastern Tribes |
| Pahasaheman | A rough game with similarities to both soccer and football.  Men played against women.  Women were allowed to tackle men and to throw the ball.  Men had to kick the ball and couldn't tackle women. | Delaware |
| Patol | Two or four players took turns throwing stone dice.  Unlike most gambling games, this was a popular spectator sport played in front of large crowds. | Southwestern Tribes |
| High Kick | A game played indoors in the winter.  Players tried to kick a sack that was suspended from the roof on a string.  The sack was raised higher each round. | Inuit |
| Hoop and Pole | This was a game that used hunting and warrior skills.  Players tried to throw a lance or spear through a rolling hoop. | Tribes universally played this game. |
| Blowgun | Contestants blew darts through a long tube.  They competed for distance and accuracy. | Cherokee |

# Native American Games and Sports *(cont.)*

**After reading the story, answer the questions.  Circle the correct answer.**

1. Why did Renaud do research on Native American games?
    a. He heard that lacrosse was originally played by Native Americans.
    b. His teammates wanted him to do the research.
    c. His coach told him to do the research.
    d. He had to if he wanted to join the school lacrosse team.

2. How was the game of Patol different from other gambling games?
    a. It was played in front of large crowds.
    b. It was played by women only.
    c. It was played by throwing dice through a hoop.
    d. It was played indoors.

3. This passage could also be called—
    a. "Women Against Men"
    b. "Pahsaheman and High Kick"
    c. "Renaud's Research"
    d. "Renaud and the Coach"

4. Information in this passage suggests that—
    a. Renaud will play high kick when lacrosse season ends
    b. lacrosse is more popular at Renaud's school than archery
    c. some tribes still play traditional Native American games
    d. Renaud's coach is a Native American lacrosse player

5. This passage was written to—
    a. show that some games involved hunting and warrior skills
    b. explain why Native Americans don't play games in winter
    c. show that there are many different Native American tribes
    d. explain several different Native American games

6. A good way to find out more about Native American games is to—
    a. watch a program about Native American baskets
    b. read a book about Native American sports
    c. talk to someone who plays lacrosse
    d. join a basketball team

# Family Name Origins

Tracing the origin of your family name can be interesting. You can learn more than just who your ancestors were. You might also find out what they did!

In Europe, family names were first used in twelfth-century England. In that time, people were often called by what their job was. If a baker were named John, he became John Baker. A professional with a bow and arrow took the name Archer. Barber was the name given to the man who cut hair.

Does your family name come from the work one of your relatives did long ago?

| Last Name | Occupation | Origins |
|---|---|---|
| Black | Dyer | Men named Black were cloth dyers who specialized in black dyes. In those days, all cloth was originally white, so it had to be dyed different colors. |
| Chandler | Candlemaker | The French word chandelier refers to a person who makes candles. |
| Fisher | Fisherman | People named Fisher were professional fishermen. |
| Gardiner | Gardener | This is a variation of the Norman word gardinier, meaning "gardener." |
| Kemp (Kempe) | Wrestler | There were unusually strong fellows who wrestled for a living. The name comes from the Old English word cempa, meaning "warrior." |
| Leach | Doctor | Leach comes from the French word laece, meaning "doctor." Medieval doctors also used blood-sucking worms called leeches on their patients. They believed these worms would purify the patient's blood and rid them of disease. |
| Smith | Metalworker | Anyone who worked with metal was called a smith. This name was originally a friendly nickname referring to the person or his business. Eventually, it became one of the most popular English names. |
| Wall | Mason | Wall was the name given to a special kind of mason— one who had great speed and skill in building wall structures. |

# Family Name Origins *(cont.)*

**After reading the story, answer the questions. Circle the correct answer.**

1. People interested in their family names should—
   a. study 12th-century England
   b. study last names beginning with the same letter
   c. find out who their ancestors were and what they did
   d. look in a book about occupations

2. You can often recognize an ancestor's occupation by—
   a. who his or her mother was
   b. his or her last name
   c. where he or she lived
   d. his or her first name

3. What is the main idea of the chart?
   a. The chart explains the origin of last names that are colors.
   b. The chart tells about the most popular family names of 12th-century England.
   c. The chart translates European words into English.
   d. The chart gives some family names and tells about the origins of those names.

4. According to this passage, the family name Taylor might mean the ancestor was a person who—
   a. traveled a lot
   b. made and sold furniture
   c. sailed boats
   d. sewed and repaired clothing

5. Information in this passage suggests that if your family name is Smith, your ancestors probably—
   a. made things out of metal
   b. cared for plants and lawns
   c. colored white cloth black
   d. built very strong walls

6. The author gives the reader reason to believe that—
   a. the name Leach came from a method to purify blood
   b. a chandler dug channels in rivers
   c. dyers wore black cloth to work and around town
   d. kemps were unusually tall men

# Cork Races

Twin brothers Aaron and Logan were always racing each other. Who could dress the quickest, who could rake leaves the fastest, who could fly a paper airplane the farthest? Today they are going to see who has the fastest cork.

Did you know that you can use the reaction between baking soda and vinegar to create a racing game? Here's how:

**Supplies:**

- one clear plastic tube about 3' long and 1" in diameter
- one painted cork ball about ¾ " diameter or small enough to easily pass through the tube
- vinegar
- dishwashing liquid
- baking soda
- measuring spoons and cup
- small container with pour spout
- tape
- baking sheet or tray

**What To Do:**

*Step 1:* Completely tape up one end of each tube to serve as the bottom.

*Step 2:* Stand tube upright on a baking sheet or tray with the taped end on the sheet. Pour 1 tablespoon of baking soda into the tube.

*Step 3:* Drop a cork into tube.

*Step 4:* Make a mixture of ½ cup of vinegar and some dishwashing liquid in the spouted container.

*Step 5:* Pour the mix carefully down the inside of one tube and watch the cork ride the suds to the top.

**Caution:** Keep your face away from the top of the tube to avoid being splashed!

**What Happened:**

The baking soda reacted with the vinegar in the mixture and produced carbon dioxide gas ($CO_2$). As the gas was released, it bubbled through the dishwashing liquid, creating the suds that pushed the cork to the top.

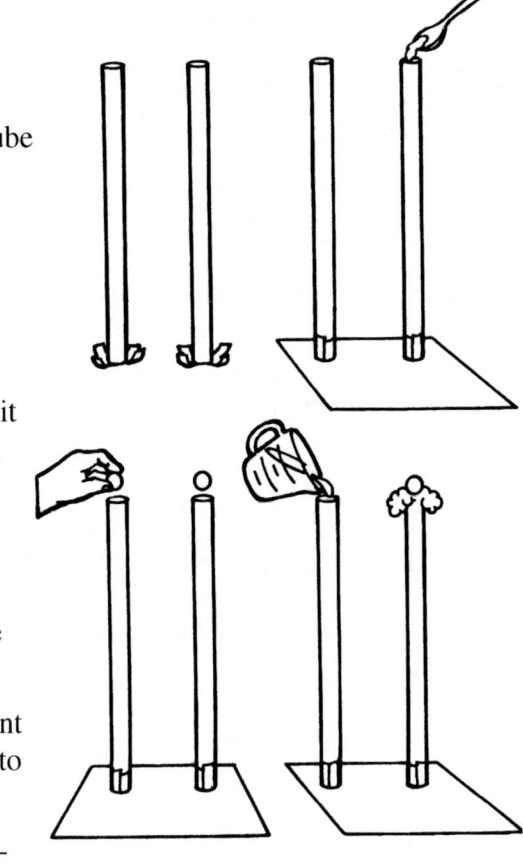

**Other Things to Try:**

- Experiment with different amounts of vinegar, baking soda, and dishwashing liquid; then have races to find the mix that makes the fastest cork.
- Mark the tubes about ⅔ of the way to the top. Experiment with mixes and quantities to get the cork to stop closest to the mark.
- Instead of a cork ball, use a wider tube and drop in Ping-Pong balls.

# Cork Races *(cont.)*

**After reading the story, answer the questions.  Circle the correct answer.**

1. The reason the cork ball rises to the top of the tube is that—
   a. the end of the tube is taped closed
   b. a cork ball is very light
   c. the suds push the balls up
   d. baking soda makes things rise

2. What might happen if you do not use vinegar?
   a. No carbon dioxide will be produced.
   b. The cork ball will still rise upward.
   c. Too much carbon dioxide will be produced.
   d. The dishwashing liquid and baking soda will produce bubbles.

3. Which of the following would not work well for this experiment?
   a. A piece of garden hose
   b. A drinking glass
   c. A paper towel roll
   d. Clear rubber tubing

4. In order to win a cork race, the directions suggest—
   a. changing the amounts of ingredients
   b. shaking up the tube
   c. using wider tubes
   d. removing the tape on the end of the tube

5. Why did the author include the first paragraph?
   a. To tell about twin brothers Aaron and Logan
   b. To explain how to have a cork race
   c. To show how to fly a paper airplane
   d. To explain what a cork race is

6. Where might you best gather most of the supplies needed for this experiment?
   a. the garage
   b. the backyard
   c. the kitchen
   d. the dining room

# A Day at the Zoo

Evelyn and her mom planned to spend the day together. Mom said, "I thought we could go to the zoo. We could take a picnic and eat lunch on the grass at the zoo."

"The zoo would be fun," Evelyn said. She looked out the window. The sun was shining. It was a beautiful summer day. They hadn't been to the zoo together in a year. The last time they went to the zoo, it was also summer.

Mom said, "Your dad needs the car. We can take the bus."

"The bus? When do we catch it?"

Mom reached in a desk drawer. She pulled out a folded piece of paper. "This is the bus schedule," she said. "It looks like the bus comes once an hour. We can catch it just a few blocks from here."

Evelyn looked at the schedule. They lived on Luther Road. It would be easy to take the bus.

## Bus #40 Weekday Schedule

| Arrivals | | | | | |
|---|---|---|---|---|---|
| Luther Road | 6:45 a.m. | 7:45 a.m. | 8:45 a.m. | 9:45 a.m. | 10:45 a.m. |
| Maple Street | 7:00 a.m. | 8:00 a.m. | 9:00 a.m. | 10:00 a.m. | 11:00 a.m. |
| 23rd Ave. | 9:27 a.m. | 10:27 a.m. | 11:27 a.m. | 12:27 p.m. | 1:27 p.m. |
| City Zoo | 10:29 a.m. | 11:29 a.m. | 12:29 p.m. | 1:29 p.m. | 2:29 p.m. |
| **Departures** | | | | | |
| City Zoo | 12:15 p.m. | 1:15 p.m. | 2:15 p.m. | 3:15 p.m. | 4:15 p.m. |
| 23rd Ave. | 1:20 p.m. | 2:20 p.m. | 3:20 p.m. | 4:20 p.m. | 5:20 p.m. |
| Maple Street | 4:15 p.m. | 5:15 p.m. | 6:15 p.m. | 7:15 p.m. | 8:15 p.m. |
| Luther Road | 4:30 p.m. | 5:30 p.m. | 6:30 p.m. | 7:30 p.m. | 8:30 p.m. |

# A Day at the Zoo *(cont.)*

**After reading the story, answer the questions.**

1. How did Evelyn and her mother get to the zoo?
   - a. walked
   - b. car
   - c. train
   - d. bus

2. The bus schedule could be used to help answer which of the following questions?
   - a. Where is the Luther Road bus stop?
   - b. How much does the City Zoo cost?
   - c. Is the transit center downtown?
   - d. How long will it take to get to the zoo?

3. Based on the passage, what might Evelyn and her mother do?
   - a. change their minds and go swimming
   - b. go to the zoo again next summer
   - c. call the bus company to find the nearest bus stop
   - d. go to the zoo on a day when Evelyn's father can join them

4. Which of these best describes Evelyn and her mother?
   - a. They don't like riding the bus.
   - b. They think the bus schedule is too complicated.
   - c. They prefer going with large groups to places.
   - d. They enjoy doing things together.

5. About how long has it been since Evelyn and her mother have been to the zoo?
   - a. one month
   - b. one year
   - c. six months
   - d. one week

6. Why did Evelyn and her mother take the bus?
   - a. her dad needed the car
   - b. her mother didn't drive
   - c. the car was out of gas
   - d. the bus was the only way to get to the zoo

# A Trip to the Video Store

Lucy and Becky went to the video store to rent videos. They had a few videos to return, too. They had videos that were five days late! They hoped that the fees would not cost them too much money. When they got to the video store, they looked at the sign that explained the fees. Here is the sign.

## Rental Fees

| | |
|---|---|
| New Releases | $2.49/day |
| Classic Favorites | $.99/day |
| Manager's Special | $1.50/day |
| Community Education | Complimentary |
| New Videos for Sale | As marked |

## Used Videos For Sale

| | |
|---|---|
| Orange Sale Sticker | 50% off original price |
| Blue Sale Sticker | 35% off original price |
| White Sale Sticker | 15% off original price |

## Special Rental Packages

Rent 10 New Release Rentals in Advance
Get 2 New Release Rentals Free

Rent 25 New Release Rentals in Advance
Get 4 New Release Rentals Free

Rent 52 Classic or New Release Rentals in Advance
Get 10 Classic or New Rentals Free

- **Late fees will accrue in accordance with daily rates.**
- **Movies due in store by 5:00 p.m. on due day. After 5:00 p.m. late fines are charged.**

# A Trip to the Video Store *(cont.)*

**After reading the story, answer the questions.**

1. What does a white sticker on a video mean?
    a. 35% off the sale price
    b. As marked
    c. 15% off the original price
    d. No Charge

2. A sign at the video store says "late fees will accrue in accordance with daily rates." The word *accrue* probably means
    a. increase
    b. decrease
    c. decline
    d. reduce

3. What important lesson might Lucy and Becky have learned when they got to the video store?
    a. They should have returned their videos on time.
    b. They shouldn't return videos if they are late.
    c. Late fines don't add up.
    d. Don't rent videos.

4. If the girls have $10.00 to spend on video rentals, how many "Classic Favorites" could they rent?
    a. 6
    b. 8
    c. 10
    d. 12

5. Instead of renting the movies, the girls decided to buy new videos. The videos have no stickers on them. Therefore they can buy the videos for
    a. half price
    b. full price
    c. 35% off
    d. 15% off

6. Community Education videos are complimentary. This is probably because
    a. they are exciting
    b. they are useful in explaining or teaching many things
    c. they describe things in a very pretty way
    d. they are action packed videos

**Directions:** Read this story carefully. When you are completely finished, answer the questions on the next page. Make sure to completely fill in the bubbles.

# An Experience Abroad

The sky was gray on Melissa's first day of school in London. Her family would be living in England for the whole year. Melissa walked to school. As she walked to school, she watched the cars on the road. In each car, the driver sat on the opposite side of the car from where drivers sit in cars in the United States. Everything about London was different than it was at home. The city had public buses, and the buses were bright red and double-decker! Still, most people used the underground subway system. They called the subway "The Tube." At home, in the U.S., Melissa rarely took the public bus and her town didn't have anything like an underground subway system. Girls in London dressed differently from the way Melissa's friends dressed back home. She looked at the girls' black skirts and stockings, their sweaters and flat shoes, and felt awkward in her own jeans and tennis shoes. Some of the girls wore jeans, but the outfits still didn't look the same as the way Melissa dressed. She was worried about the first day of school.

Melissa was afraid that she wouldn't know anything and wouldn't make any friends. Even though everyone was speaking English, sometimes Melissa still had trouble understanding because there was more than one type of accent in England. She had to listen very closely. How could she make friends if she couldn't understand the accent?

The sidewalk under Melissa's feet wasn't made of cement the way it would have been at home. It was made of an endless number of bricks set in the earth. Sometimes the bricks jutted up at angles and Melissa felt them hit her feet unevenly. The sidewalk looked like it was a hundred years old. The only trees Melissa saw were very young and thin, more like potted plants than real trees. Back home, she lived on a street that was covered with big, full-grown trees.

Melissa reached her new school. There were students sitting outside on the school steps and standing in clusters on the sidewalk. Some students were entering the building. Other students were waiting until the last minute to go inside. The school building, like the sidewalk, was also made of red brick. It too, looked very old. It looked nothing like Melissa's school back home.

Melissa took a piece of paper from her pocket and unfolded it. This piece of paper told her where to find her new classroom. She told herself not to be nervous and she went inside. When she found the classroom, she quickly sat in the first available desk.

"Welcome," the teacher said. "Class, this is our new student, Melissa, from the United States." The teacher smiled. Then he said, "Let's introduce ourselves and maybe ask Melissa a few questions about her home town."

Melissa worried that they might ask difficult questions, like the exact number of the population. She tried to remember her state song.

One girl raised her hand. She introduced herself as Rita, then asked, "Does the United States look the way it does on the telly?"

# An Experience Abroad *(cont.)*

Melissa knew "telly" meant television. She said, "Well, that depends on which television shows you watch, I guess."

Everybody laughed and Melissa knew she was turning bright red with embarrassment. Then she realized they weren't laughing at her. They were laughing because they thought her answer was meant to be funny! They thought she was clever.

A boy raised his hand. He said his name was Simon. He asked, "Do you live close to Hollywood?"

Melissa explained that Hollywood was a long distance away from her hometown. Then she said, "But I have been there. Once, on vacation, I toured the Hollywood studios with my grandmother."

She spoke slowly and clearly. She didn't want the students to have trouble with her accent.

One girl raised her hand. She said, "I love your outfit. It looks so much like the pictures in American magazines."

Melissa was surprised. She said, "Why, thank you." As Melissa answered questions, she realized that instead of knowing nothing, in at least one way she was an expert. She knew more about the United States than anyone else in the classroom!

# An Experience Abroad (cont.)

1. What is the best summary of the first paragraph?
   a) Melissa felt anxious about taking a public bus and using the underground subway system.
   b) Melissa missed her friends at school back in the United States.
   c) Melissa worried about her first day of school in London because things seemed so different from the United States.
   d) Melissa wasn't sure she wanted to dress in black skirts and stockings.

2. According to the passage, some of the bricks jutted up at angles. This description means that some of the bricks—
   a) stuck out      b) crumbled      c) sparkled      d) eroded away

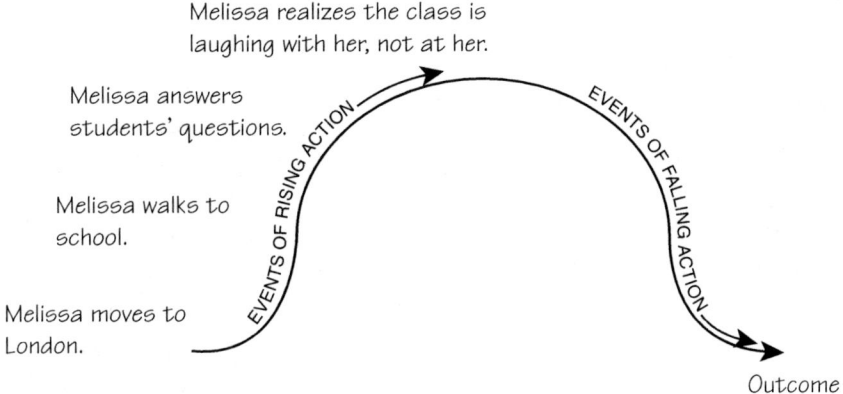

3. Which of these belongs to the area marked "Events of Falling Action"?
   a) Melissa notices the styles of clothes the students wear.
   b) Melissa checks the paper for her classroom.
   c) The teacher welcomes Melissa to the class.
   d) A student gives Melissa a compliment on her outfit.

4. How will Melissa be different as a result of living in London for a year?
   a) She will know more about another culture.
   b) She will know how to speak a new language.
   c) She will never wear jeans and tennis shoes again.
   d) She will be reluctant to answer questions about London.

5. What opinion did Melissa have of London as she walked to school?
   a) A foreign language was very difficult to understand.
   b) There were some surprising similarities between London and home.
   c) Everything about London was different from the way it was at home.
   d) The girls on their way to school looked just like girls back home.

6. This story can best be described as—
   a) fiction
   b) a fable
   c) historical fiction
   d) science fiction

**Directions:** Read this story carefully. When you are completely finished, answer the questions on the next page. Make sure to completely fill in the bubbles.

# U.S. Camel Corps

Before there were cars, people in America used horses to travel. They either rode in a saddle on a horse's back or used several horses to pull a wagon. Taxis were even pulled by horses. Horses were used to plow fields, to pull heavy logs, and even to pull boats. But horses didn't work well in the deserts of the American Southwest. Horses need lots of water, which was hard to find in the desert. And horses have hooves that made it hard for them to walk in deep sand. Also, horses can't eat many plants that grow in the desert. Special food had to be brought to the desert for them to eat.

All of this created problems for the cavalry, the division of the army that used horses. Because the cavalry had trouble using horses in the desert, someone came up with the idea for the cavalry to use camels instead. That is how the U.S. Camel Corps was born.

Camels have no problem living in the desert. They have broad, flat feet that are perfect for walking over deep sand. They have special eyelids that keep blowing sand out of their eyes. But the most important thing to know about camels is that they can go for a long time without water. That is why people have used camels to travel through deserts for thousands of years.

At first, the cavalry wasn't sure what kind of camels to use. There are two kinds of camels. It is easy to tell the two kinds apart by looking at their humps. The humps are where camels store extra fat that they use to survive on long trips through the desert. Dromedary camels have one hump. They live in

the hot deserts of the Middle East in countries like Jordan and Egypt. Bactrian camels have two humps. They live in deserts that are sometimes cold, like the mountains of Afghanistan and in Mongolia. The cavalry finally decided to use dromedary camels because they were better suited for the hot summers in the southwestern U.S.

The cavalry formed the U.S. Camel Corps. They brought 34 camels to America from North Africa in a ship named *Supply.* But no one in the new U.S. Camel Corps had ever worked with camels. They didn't know what camels ate or how to take care of them. They also discovered that camels have bad tempers and can be hard to handle. The cavalry hired an expert from Syria named Hadji Ali to teach them about camels. Hadji Ali had years of experience with camels and taught the Americans how to use and care for the animals.

The camels were used on several trips between Texas and California. They worked great. Not only could they live in the desert, they could also carry four times as many supplies as a horse.

But the camels were just too strange for most Americans. The camels also scared the horses. This is why the U.S. Camel Corps came to an end after only a few years. The army canceled the program, and the camels were sold off to circuses and private individuals. However, some of the camels escaped. For many years, people living in the desert reported seeing strange animals living there that may have been camels.

# U.S. Camel Corps *(cont.)*

1. Why did the cavalry use camels in the deserts of the Southwest?
   - (a) There were not enough horses to go around.
   - (b) Camels were better suited to the desert than horses.
   - (c) Camels would be frightening to the enemy.
   - (d) Camels were easy to obtain.

2. Why is the desert a difficult place for a horse?
   - (a) A horse cannot tolerate the heat.
   - (b) There is not enough water.
   - (c) The desert ground is too hard.
   - (d) A horse can easily lose its way in a desert.

3. What is another good title for this passage?
   - (a) "Camels Forever"
   - (b) "Desert Sands"
   - (c) "Short-Term Camels"
   - (d) "Horses in the Desert"

4. According to the passage, camels must be—
   - (a) raised away from people
   - (b) kept in their native habitats
   - (c) treated differently from horses
   - (d) kept in zoos to survive

5. Why did the author include the last paragraph?
   - (a) To describe some differences between horses and camels
   - (b) To explain how people felt about the end of the U.S. Camel Corps
   - (c) So the reader would understand why camels stopped being used by the U.S. Cavalry
   - (d) To tell why no one liked the use of camels in the cavalry

6. Which words tell you that the cavalry did not know much about camels?
   - (a) Camels can go for a long time without water.
   - (b) Camels have no problem living in the desert.
   - (c) The cavalry finally decided to use dromedary camels.
   - (d) No one in the U.S. Camel Corps had ever worked with camels.

**Directions:** Read this story carefully. When you are completely finished, answer the questions on the next page. Make sure to completely fill in the bubbles.

# Emergency Procedures

## Severe Weather

Severe weather may include unusually cold, windy, or snowy conditions.

*General Winter Storm Safety Rules:*

- Listen to the radio or television for weather updates.

*Dress Wisely:*

- Layers of thin clothing are warmer than single layers of thick clothing.
- Mittens are warmer than gloves.
- Wear a hat; most body heat is lost through the top of the head.
- Cover your mouth to protect your lungs from cold air.
- A winter storm **Watch** means that severe winter weather conditions may affect the area. This could mean freezing rain, sleet or heavy snow. If a winter storm **Watch** is issued for the area:

  ☆ Avoid unnecessary travel before or during the severe weather.

- A winter storm Warning means that severe weather (freezing rain, sleet or heavy snow) is about to occur. If a Warning is issued for the area:

  ☆ Stay indoors during the storm; avoid travel.

*Avoid traveling by car in a storm, but if you must:*

- Keep your car's gas tank full for emergency use and to keep the fuel line from freezing.
- Let someone know where you are going and when you expect to arrive.
- Have emergency supplies in the trunk, including blankets.

*If you do get stuck:*

- Stay with your car. **Do not try** to walk to safety.
- Tie a brightly colored cloth (preferably a red one) to the antenna for rescuers to see.
- Leave the overhead light on so that you can be seen.
- As you sit, keep moving your arms and legs to keep blood circulating and to stay warm.
- Keep one window slightly open to let in air.
- Use your heater sparingly. Keep the exhaust pipe clear so fumes won't back up into the car.

# Emergency Procedures *(cont.)*

1. The author probably wrote this bulletin to
   - (a) advise people what to do in severe weather.
   - (b) explain how to drive in snow and ice.
   - (c) describe how a storm is formed.
   - (d) warn people to dress properly.

2. Information in this bulletin shows that it is
   - (a) an advertisement.
   - (b) a short story.
   - (c) a public service announcement.
   - (d) a community class schedule.

3. What is the overall meaning of this bulletin?
   - (a) The public does not need to take a storm warning seriously.
   - (b) A storm watch and a storm warning are both serious.
   - (c) A storm watch will become a storm warning.
   - (d) Have layers of thin clothing on hand at all times.

4. If you heard about a storm watch, what would this mean?
   - (a) There will soon be a storm.
   - (b) Do not travel during a storm watch.
   - (c) People should stock up on emergency supplies.
   - (d) A storm is possible.

5. This bulletin advises people to move their arms to keep blood circulating. Which of these words means the same as *circulating*?
   - (a) moving
   - (b) blushing
   - (c) freezing
   - (d) gusting

6. Which of these is *not* a way to keep warm?
   - (a) take off your hat
   - (b) dress in layers
   - (c) move your arms and legs
   - (d) wear mittens instead of gloves

# Practice Answer Sheet

This sheet may be reproduced and used with the reading comprehension questions. Each box can be used with one story. Using the answer sheets with the stories and questions gives extra practice in test preparation.

| Page 5 | Page 7 | Page 9 |
|---|---|---|
| 1. (a) (b) (c) (d) | 1. (a) (b) (c) (d) | 1. (a) (b) (c) (d) |
| 2. (a) (b) (c) (d) | 2. (a) (b) (c) (d) | 2. (a) (b) (c) (d) |
| 3. (a) (b) (c) (d) | 3. (a) (b) (c) (d) | 3. (a) (b) (c) (d) |
| 4. (a) (b) (c) (d) | 4. (a) (b) (c) (d) | 4. (a) (b) (c) (d) |
| 5. (a) (b) (c) (d) | 5. (a) (b) (c) (d) | 5. (a) (b) (c) (d) |
| 6. (a) (b) (c) (d) | 6. (a) (b) (c) (d) | 6. (a) (b) (c) (d) |
| **Page 11** | **Page 13** | **Page 16** |
| 1. (a) (b) (c) (d) | 1. (a) (b) (c) (d) | 1. (a) (b) (c) (d) |
| 2. (a) (b) (c) (d) | 2. (a) (b) (c) (d) | 2. (a) (b) (c) (d) |
| 3. (a) (b) (c) (d) | 3. (a) (b) (c) (d) | 3. (a) (b) (c) (d) |
| 4. (a) (b) (c) (d) | 4. (a) (b) (c) (d) | 4. (a) (b) (c) (d) |
| 5. (a) (b) (c) (d) | 5. (a) (b) (c) (d) | 5. (a) (b) (c) (d) |
| 6. (a) (b) (c) (d) | 6. (a) (b) (c) (d) | 6. (a) (b) (c) (d) |
| **Page 18** | **Page 20** | **Page 22** |
| 1. (a) (b) (c) (d) | 1. (a) (b) (c) (d) | 1. (a) (b) (c) (d) |
| 2. (a) (b) (c) (d) | 2. (a) (b) (c) (d) | 2. (a) (b) (c) (d) |
| 3. (a) (b) (c) (d) | 3. (a) (b) (c) (d) | 3. (a) (b) (c) (d) |
| 4. (a) (b) (c) (d) | 4. (a) (b) (c) (d) | 4. (a) (b) (c) (d) |
| 5. (a) (b) (c) (d) | 5. (a) (b) (c) (d) | 5. (a) (b) (c) (d) |
| 6. (a) (b) (c) (d) | 6. (a) (b) (c) (d) | 6. (a) (b) (c) (d) |

# Practice Answer Sheet *(cont.)*

| Page 24 | Page 26 | Page 28 |
|---|---|---|
| 1. (a) (b) (c) (d) | 1. (a) (b) (c) (d) | 1. (a) (b) (c) (d) |
| 2. (a) (b) (c) (d) | 2. (a) (b) (c) (d) | 2. (a) (b) (c) (d) |
| 3. (a) (b) (c) (d) | 3. (a) (b) (c) (d) | 3. (a) (b) (c) (d) |
| 4. (a) (b) (c) (d) | 4. (a) (b) (c) (d) | 4. (a) (b) (c) (d) |
| 5. (a) (b) (c) (d) | 5. (a) (b) (c) (d) | 5. (a) (b) (c) (d) |
| 6. (a) (b) (c) (d) | 6. (a) (b) (c) (d) | 6. (a) (b) (c) (d) |

| Page 30 | Page 32 | Page 34 |
|---|---|---|
| 1. (a) (b) (c) (d) | 1. (a) (b) (c) (d) | 1. (a) (b) (c) (d) |
| 2. (a) (b) (c) (d) | 2. (a) (b) (c) (d) | 2. (a) (b) (c) (d) |
| 3. (a) (b) (c) (d) | 3. (a) (b) (c) (d) | 3. (a) (b) (c) (d) |
| 4. (a) (b) (c) (d) | 4. (a) (b) (c) (d) | 4. (a) (b) (c) (d) |
| 5. (a) (b) (c) (d) | 5. (a) (b) (c) (d) | 5. (a) (b) (c) (d) |
| 6. (a) (b) (c) (d) | 6. (a) (b) (c) (d) | 6. (a) (b) (c) (d) |

| Page 36 | Page 38 |
|---|---|
| 1. (a) (b) (c) (d) | 1. (a) (b) (c) (d) |
| 2. (a) (b) (c) (d) | 2. (a) (b) (c) (d) |
| 3. (a) (b) (c) (d) | 3. (a) (b) (c) (d) |
| 4. (a) (b) (c) (d) | 4. (a) (b) (c) (d) |
| 5. (a) (b) (c) (d) | 5. (a) (b) (c) (d) |
| 6. (a) (b) (c) (d) | 6. (a) (b) (c) (d) |

# Answer Key

**Branding Day, page 5**
1. d
2. a
3. d
4. d
5. b
6. d

**Dad's Haircut, page 7**
1. a
2. a
3. a
4. a
5. c
6. b

**Grandpa's Plane, page 9**
1. d
2. a
3. a
4. b
5. c
6. c

**The Rock Hound, page 11**
1. b
2. d
3. a
4. a
5. a
6. d

**The Perfect Picture, page 13**
1. b
2. b
3. c
4. b
5. a
6. c

**Lester's Find, page 16**
1. d
2. c
3. a
4. b
5. a
6. a

**Keyboard Master, page 18**
1. d
2. c
3. a
4. c
5. a
6. d

**Birth of an Island, page 20**
1. a
2. a
3. b
4. c
5. c
6. c

**Grizzlies, page 22**
1. c
2. b
3. d
4. a
5. d
6. a

**For the Record, page 24**
1. b
2. b
3. b
4. b
5. c
6. c

**Building a Medieval Castle, page 26**
1. c
2. b
3. a
4. a
5. c
6. d

**David Scott-Risner, page 28**
1. d
2. a
3. c
4. a
5. c
6. a

**Native American Games and Sports, page 30**
1. a
2. a
3. c
4. c
5. d
6. b

**Family Name Origins, page 32**
1. c
2. b
3. d

4. d
5. a
6. a

**Cork Races, page 34**
1. c
2. a
3. c
4. a
5. b
6. c

**A Day at the Zoo, page 36**
1. d
2. d
3. b
4. d
5. b
6. a

**A Trip to the Video Store, page 38**
1. c
2. a
3. a
4. c
5. b
6. b

**An Experience Abroad, page 41**
1. c
2. a
3. d
4. a
5. c
6. a

**U.S. Camel Corps, page 43**
1. b
2. b
3. c
4. c
5. c
6. d

**Emergency Procedures, page 45**
1. a
2. c
3. b
4. d
5. a
6. a